OXFORD GRADED 1
500 Headwords

The Three Goats and the Dwarf

The Horse and the Donkey

The Ant and the Dove

London
OXFORD UNIVERSITY PRESS

Oxford University Press, Ely House, London W.1

GLASGOW NEW YORK TORONTO MELBOURNE WELLINGTON
CAPE TOWN IBADAN NAIROBI DAR ES SALAAM LUSAKA ADDIS ABABA
DELHI BOMBAY CALCUTTA MADRAS KARACHI LAHORE DACCA
KUALA LUMPUR SINGAPORE HONG KONG TOKYO

© *Oxford University Press 1971*

ISBN 0 19 421709 4

First published 1971
Third impression 1975

The stories in this book are rewritten by L. A. Hill.
The Three Goats and the Dwarf has been adapted from
The Three Billy Goats Gruff (Nelson). Acknowledgement
is due to the original author, Miss P. Laflin.
The other two stories are from Aesop.
The illustrations are by Richard Kennedy.

Printed in Great Britain by
Hazell Watson & Viney Ltd
Aylesbury, Bucks

The Three Goats and the Dwarf

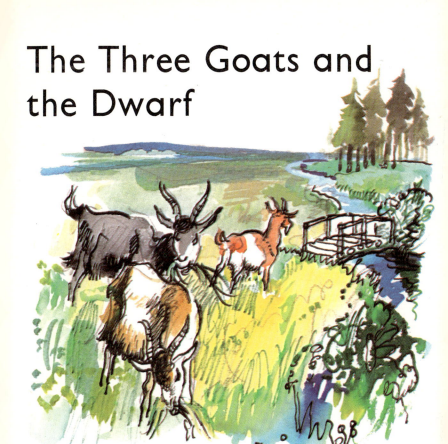

These animals are goats. They are in a field, and they are eating grass.

There is some very good grass near those trees. The smallest goat is looking at it, and he is saying, 'That grass is greener than ours. I am going to go there, and I am going to eat it.'

But there is a river between the goats and the grass, and that bridge is very narrow.

The biggest goat said,
'Do not go on that bridge.
There is a bad dwarf there.
He is behind those bushes.'

But the small goat laughed, and he said, 'I am
not afraid. The dwarf is not going to eat me,
because I am small and thin.'

He ran to the bridge, and he put his foot on it.
The dwarf came. He said,
'Who is on my bridge?'

The small goat said, 'I
am.'

The dwarf said, 'I am going to eat you,' but the goat said, 'Do not eat me. I am very small and thin. The big goats are going to come. Eat them. They are fatter.'

The dwarf looked at the big goats, and he said, 'Yes, they are fatter. I am not going to eat you. I am going to eat the big goats.'

The small goat was happy. He ran to the long, green grass, and he ate some of it.

He said, 'This grass is very good.'

2 The middle-sized goat looked at the small one, and he said, 'The dwarf did not eat him, and that grass is very green. I am going to go there too.'

He went to the bridge, and he put his foot on it. The dwarf came again, and he said, 'Who is standing on my bridge?'

The middle-sized goat said, 'I am.'

The dwarf said, 'I am going to eat you.'

But the goat said, 'No, do not eat me. I am not very big, and I am not very fat. The big goat is going to come here. Eat him. He is very fat.'

The dwarf looked at the middle-sized goat, and then he looked at the big goat. He said, 'Yes, you are not very big, and you are not very fat. I am not going to eat you. I am going to eat the big goat.'

The middle-sized goat was happy. He ran to the long, green grass, and he ate a lot of it.

3   Then the biggest goat looked at the small goat, and he looked at the middle-sized goat.

He said, 'The grass is very good there. The dwarf did not eat the small goat, and he did not eat the middle-sized goat. I am going to go there too, and I am going to eat that long, green grass.'

He went to the bridge, and he put his foot on it.

The dwarf came again, and he said, 'Who is on my bridge now?'

The big goat said, 'I am.'

The dwarf looked at him, and he was very happy. He said, 'This goat is very big, and he is very fat.'

Then he said, 'I am going to eat you.'

The big goat laughed, and he said, 'Come and catch me.'

The dwarf came near the big goat. Then he was afraid. He said, 'This is a very big, strong goat, and he has got very long horns.'

The goat ran to the dwarf, and he pushed him with his horns. The dwarf fell into the river, and the big goat laughed again.

He said, 'Are you thirsty? There is a lot of water in the river. Drink it.'

Then he ran to the long, green grass, and he ate it too.

The Horse and the Donkey

A man put two heavy bags on his old donkey, but he did not put any on his horse.

The donkey looked at the horse, and he said, 'I am very tired. Take one of these bags, and carry it.'

But the horse was angry. He said, 'I am not a donkey. I am a beautiful horse. I am not going to carry a bag.'

The donkey fell, and he died. The man took the bags, and he put both of them on the horse's back.

Then he put the dead donkey on it too. He said, 'I am going to sell the donkey's skin.'

Then the horse said, 'Why did I say, "I am not going to carry a bag?" Now the donkey has died, and I am carrying two bags and a dead donkey.'

The Ant and the Dove

This ant was thirsty.
He went to a river,
but he fell into it.
He shouted, 'Help me.
I am drowning.'

There was a dove in a tree near the river.

She took a leaf, and she threw it into the river.

The ant climbed on the leaf, and it went to the side of the river.

The ant climbed off it. He was very happy. He said, 'That is a good dove.'

Then a man came to the side of the river.
He looked at the dove, and he said, 'I am going to catch that bird.'

He took his net, and he threw it.

But the ant bit his foot, and the net fell into the river.

The dove flew out of the tree. She was very happy. She said, 'I helped the ant, and now the ant has helped me.'

The Three Goats and the Dwarf

dwarf

A **dwarf** is a very small man.

field

This is a **field**.

There are two **fields** here.

goat

This animal is a **goat**.

grass

This is **grass**. It is green.

horn
These are **horns**.

This goat has got long **horns**.

middle-sized: not big and not small.

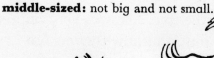

This goat is small,

this one is big,

and this one is **middle-sized**.

narrow

This bridge is **narrow**.

But this one is not **narrow**.

1. Why did the smallest goat want the grass near the trees?
2. Why did the biggest goat say, 'Do not go on that bridge'?
3. Why did the dwarf say, 'I am not going to eat the smallest goat'?
4. Why did the biggest goat go on the bridge?
5. Why was the dwarf happy then?
6. The dwarf came near the big goat. Was the dwarf happy then?
7. Was he afraid? Why?

The Horse and the Donkey

carry(ing)

This donkey is **carrying** a bag.

This man is **carrying** a basket.

dead/died

This donkey is **dead**.

skin

This is a lion's **skin,**

and this is a donkey's **skin**.

It **died yesterday**.

1. Why did the donkey say, 'Carry one of these bags'?
2. Why did the horse say, 'I am not going to carry a bag'?
3. What did the man put on the horse's back?
4. Why did he put the dead donkey on the horse?
5. What mistake did the horse make?

The Ant and the Dove

ant

This is an **ant**.

biting/bit

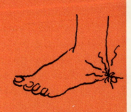

That dog is **biting** John.

The ant **bit** the man's foot yesterday.

dove

This bird is a **dove**.

drowning

This child is **drowning**.

help/helped

Help me.

The child is shouting '**Help** me.'

Now a man is going to **help** the child.

1. Why did the ant go to the river?
2. What did he do there?
3. What did the dove do?
4. What did the man bring to the side of the river?
5. Why did it fall into the river?

Draw a black ant. Draw it on a green leaf. Draw the leaf on a blue river.